NATIONAL GEOGRAPHIC
KIDS™

EVERYTHING
MONEY

NATIONAL GEOGRAPHIC
KIDS

EVERYTHING
MONEY

BY KATHY FURGANG

WITH NATIONAL GEOGRAPHIC EXPLORER FRED HIEBERT

NATIONAL
GEOGRAPHIC

WASHINGTON, D.C.

CONTENTS

Whether you run a lemonade stand that serves the neighborhood or a company that makes lemonade for millions of people, owning your own business can be challenging and rewarding.

Tourists and locals alike flock to Khao San Road in Bangkok, Thailand, where they can buy Thai handicrafts, used books, paintings, and clothing.

INTRODUCTION

KA-CHING! THAT'S THE
SOUND OF COLD HARD CASH, DOUGH, BREAD,

loot, dinero, greenbacks—whatever you want to call it, it's money, money, money.

Does the thought of a mountain of moolah make you think of all those things you could be buying right now? Are you in the market for a new video game system with the best new games to play on it? Or maybe you're in the market for some clothes, toys, a cell phone, a computer, a present for a friend, or a new bike. The list could go on forever.

Sure, you know that money can buy you *stuff,* but have you ever really thought about the money itself? What is it, and why is it valuable? Why does money from one country look so different from another country's money?

Have you heard the expression "Money makes the world go around"? In a way, it's true—we use money for just about everything, from food, to clothing, to the electricity and water inside your home. So, cash in on some knowledge and learn **EVERYTHING** about money.

EXPLORER'S CORNER

Hi, I'm archaeologist Fred Hiebert.

I've gone on digs all around the world to learn about the past. I can tell you that money dates back a long time, because I've dug up some pretty old coins! You'd be surprised to find out what we can learn about money and the things people value by looking at artifacts from the past.

Money comes in different shapes and sizes. These euro coins, which come in denominations ranging from one cent to two euros, are used in many European countries.

MONEY, MONEY, MONEY!

WHAT IS MONEY?

WE USE MONEY ALL

THE TIME, BUT WHAT IS MONEY, really? Money is something that can be used as an exchange for goods or services. We usually think of money as bills and coins, but that's not all that can be used as money. In fact, shells were used as a form of money for years. As long as both parties agree upon the form of payment, money can come in many forms.

IS IT BETTER TO BARTER?

When two traders did not use the same form of money, they bartered. Bartering is an exchange of goods or services for other goods or services. As early as 9000 B.C., people were trading cows for other things. It was useful to barter livestock because people needed animals for food, for clothing, and to help them do work. Explorers in new lands, such as the Spanish explorers in North America in the 1500s, also bartered because they did not have any local money to exchange for what they needed.

Trading a chicken for goods in the 1800s

During the Inca Empire (1438–1533), people would often barter for goods in a central marketplace.

MONEY WI$E IN 1946, HUNGARY ISSUED A 100 QUINTILLION PENGO BANKNOTE.

10 NGK EVERYTHING

MONEY VS. CURRENCY

You might hear the word *currency* when people talk about money. Currency is the system, or type, of money that a particular area or country uses. Currency in Brazil is called the real (REE al), (at top left), and currency in India is called the rupee, (at bottom left). Countries can have their own currency, or they can share a common currency. And even though it's all money, different currencies are worth different amounts.

MANY KINDS OF MONEY

In the past, people used many different things to exchange for goods or services. In addition to livestock and shells, people have used metals such as gold or copper, woven blankets, silk, fish, salt, tea leaves, peppercorn, and even bat droppings. Why? It makes a good fertilizer! On the island of Yap, Micronesia, people use giant stones called rai (at right) as a form of currency.

WHAT ISN'T MONEY?

IT ISN'T A LOAN. A loan is an agreement for one person to receive money with a promise to pay back money in the future. A loan isn't a form of money, currency, or bartering. The person who gave you the loan gave you money, but this person did not get goods in exchange. Most loans come with interest, which means you pay back the original amount of money plus some more.

IT ISN'T A CREDIT CARD. Credit cards are similar to loans. When you buy something using a credit card, you do not give the store money—the credit card company does. Each month, you pay all or part of that money back to the credit card company, plus any interest that is owed.

FROM ROCKS TO STOCKS

MONEY SURE HAS CHANGED OVER TIME.

IT'S A GOOD THING, TOO. WHO WANTS TO BE CARRYING AROUND COWS OR

shells in their pockets? And most store owners today would not be happy if you tried to pay for a video game with a handful of bat droppings. Take a walk through the past and learn about the changing face of money.

Cowrie shells

Greek and Roman coins

Bolts of silk fabric

STONE AGE	30,000 YEARS AGO	5,000 B.C.	1000 B.C.

STONE AGE TRADE

New archaeological evidence shows that stone from Africa was carried all the way to Arabia almost 165,000 years ago. Archaeologists believe the stone was traded as raw material to make tools.

30,000 YEARS AGO

Paint pigments made of ground-up minerals were exchanged in Europe. The pigments were used in paints to make pictures. The earliest paintings were made in caves, where they have been discovered and studied by archaeologists.

1200 B.C.

Cowrie shells are mollusk shells found in ocean waters, especially in the Indian Ocean. Many types of shells have been used as currency, but cowrie shells were so easily found that they became the most common shell currency in Africa and parts of China.

500 B.C.

The first **silver coins** came from the country now known as Turkey. The Greek and Roman Empires used images of gods and emperors on their silver coins.

200 B.C.

Silk was used much like money, and its trade across Asia and Europe helped ancient Rome and countries such as China and India develop and grow.

Paper money

Wampum belt

Gold bars

Modern currency exchange

NYSE

A.D. 1000   1500   2000

806 A.D.

Paper first became a form of currency in China. However, **paper money** disappeared after about 500 years. Paper money reappeared in Europe after the 1500s.

1535

Wampum means "white" or "white beads," named for the white clamshells these strings of beads were made from. Native Americans most likely used them for trading well before the first record of them in 1535.

1821

The "gold standard" means that the currency was once based on the value of **gold**. As gold increases or decreases in value, the paper money of a country becomes similarly more or less valuable. This system was used by several nations for many years, but it is no longer used today.

TODAY

Today, money is mostly currency based. Different countries handle their monetary systems differently, and the value of money even changes a bit from day to day. Today, people rely heavily on **digital transactions** to send money around the world.

WHY MONEY MATTERS

La Boqueria, a large public market in Barcelona, Spain

WHAT'S THE BIG DEAL

ABOUT MONEY? IT BUYS THE THINGS you need: food, a roof over your head, clothes on your back, and shoes on your feet. Having enough money to pay for electricity, heat, and water is necessary, too. And then there's transportation: a car, gasoline, or bus fare. When people do not have enough money to meet their basic needs, they are living in poverty.

MORE, MORE, MORE!

Ever wonder why people who already have money want more of it? People are often motivated by the possibility of having more in life—a bigger home, new designer clothes, or an expensive sports car. People also earn extra money to help plan for the future. A college education and retirement are some things that people take years to save money for.

MONEY WI$E IF YOU SPENT ONE DOLLAR EVERY SECOND OF EVERY DAY, YOU WOULD SPEND $31,536,000 IN ONE YEAR.

By the Numbers

1% of Americans earn more than $300,000 each year.

13% of people around the world don't have enough to eat.

27% of people in Greece live in poverty.

30% is the average amount of each paycheck that people in China save.

47% of Russian people say that they own a car.

80% is the percentage of income an average U.S. household spends out of what it earns.

DOES MONEY = POWER?

Many rich people have power. They can buy anything they want and even hire people to do things for them. Rich corporations can influence what people do or buy. But there are many powerful things people do with no money. Inventing things and helping others allow people to have power over their own lives.

WHAT MONEY CAN'T BUY

Money can buy a lot of things, but it certainly can't buy everything. For example, money can buy a gift for a friend, but it can't buy a good friend. It can buy a college education, but it can't buy intelligence or common sense. It can buy a diamond engagement ring, but it can't buy true love. Many of life's best experiences are free!

MAKING MONEY

MONEY DOESN'T
GROW ON TREES, AS THEY SAY.

Banknotes, or paper money, are made at a country's central, or national, bank. Some countries, such as the United States, Canada, and Japan, print their own currency. Other countries, such as those in the European Union, share the responsibility of printing their currency, the euro.

Coins are made at a place called a mint. The world's largest mint is in Philadelphia, Pennsylvania, U.S.A. It mints tons of coins each year. In the United States, between 11 billion and 20 billion coins are produced annually. The first mint in the United States opened in 1792.

MONEY WI$E IT COSTS $1.67 TO MAKE A DOLLAR'S WORTH OF PENNIES.

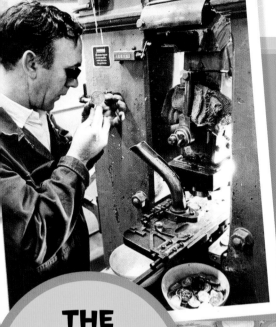

The Royal Mint in England makes coins for 60 countries. The history of the mint goes back some 1,100 years. In the photo (at left), a worker inspects a New Zealand decimal coin. In 1967, the New Zealand government replaced its pound, which was made up of 20 shillings, or 240 pence, with the New Zealand dollar, which was made up of 100 cents. The new currency was more convenient to use.

SHABBY MONEY

In some countries, such as the United States, the United Kingdom, and South Africa, you can have a ripped or damaged bill replaced. In the United States, if you have more than half of the bill, bring it to any local bank. If you have less than half of it, send it to the U.S. Treasury Department for a replacement. Back in 1916, you could take your money to Washington, D.C., to get it washed, ironed, and reissued for free!

THE COLOR OF MONEY

Around the world, 180 countries print bills in different sizes and colors!

AUSTRALIA
WAS THE
FIRST COUNTRY
TO USE
PLASTIC BILLS.

MAKING MONEY

Paper currency, such as the Turkish lira (at left), is first printed onto giant rolls attached to a printing press. After they are printed, the rolls of money are cut into sheets of money, which are then cut again to make the individual bills we spend at the store.

A PHOTOGRAPHIC DIAGRAM

Color-Shifting Ink

The 100 in the corner looks black, but shift it slightly and it turns a swamp-green color. The special ink is a top-secret formula sold only to the U.S. government, and it cannot be photocopied or duplicated.

HOW DO YOU SPOT

A FAKE? NATIONAL BANKS GO TO great lengths to make it difficult to counterfeit currency. First, the paper that money is printed on isn't made from trees. It is made from a blend of cotton and linen, with different colors of ink used throughout. This material makes the bills more durable than regular paper and more difficult to duplicate. Many countries make it difficult to counterfeit. For example, some Canadian 20-dollar bills feature a see-through number. Half of the number 20 appears on the front of the bill and the other half appears on the back. When you hold up the bill to the light, you can see the whole numeral.

Look closely at this U.S. 100-dollar bill and you'll see some tricks used to outsmart the bad guys.

Patriotic Fibers

Dollar bills have red and blue fibers (like the American flag!) randomly embedded in them. This gives the bill a distinctive texture, and the fibers are difficult to duplicate.

Jagged Edges

Use a magnifying glass to look at the Federal Reserve and Treasury seals. The saw-toothed edges are sharp and clear.

Fine Engraving Lines

The image of U.S. statesman Benjamin Franklin is so detailed with engraving lines that the lines will become distorted if it is copied or scanned.

Portraits That Pop

Look carefully at the portrait of Franklin, especially his face. Bills are designed so that portraits look three-dimensional, not flat.

3-D Security Ribbon

Hold the bill up to a light and you can see a 3-D security strip woven into the bill from top to bottom. The bells and 100s on the strip will move from side to side when the bill is tilted. Under a black light, the strip will glow pink.

Watermark

A watermark is a very faint design embedded into paper when it is made. Hold the bill up to a light and you will see a watermark of a second portrait of Franklin to the right of the large one.

Made in America

The phrase "United States of America" is micro-printed on the collar of Franklin's jacket.

Magic Inkwell

Look for an image of a brown quill inkwell. If you tilt the bill, you will see a bell inside the inkwell that changes from copper to green. The bell appears and disappears as the bill is tilted.

Tiny Printing

The thin lines on the bill look like engraver's marks, but if you magnify the bill many times you will see the words "USA 100" printed over and over again inside the 100 in the corner, which is less than half an inch tall.

The ice-cream truck rings its bell and kids dash out of their houses to buy their favorite cones and ice pops. We all make decisions every day about which treats are worth spending our precious stash of cash on.

2
MONEY IN, MONEY OUT

THE LIFE OF MONEY

YOU PULL MONEY OUT OF YOUR POCKET TO PAY

FOR A SNACK AT THE SCHOOL LUNCH COUNTER. WHERE DID THAT MONEY COME FROM, and where does it go next? It's somewhere on its way in a long journey from the government bank that printed it to the thousands of people who passed it around. Take a look at just one possible journey that currency can take.

1 Mrs. Coyne gets a $10 bill from her bank account.

2 Mrs. Coyne pays Billy the $10 for washing her car.

3 Billy uses the $10 bill to help him buy a video game.

4 The cashier, Mr. Schilling, gives the $10 bill to the next customer, Penny, as change when she makes a purchase.

5 Penny gives the $10 as a gift in a birthday card to her niece, Goldie.

6 Goldie puts her $10 in the bank. She is saving money for a new camera.

MONEY WI$E RESPECT THE BILL. IN AUSTRALIA, CANADA, AND THE UNITED STATES, IT IS A CRIME TO BURN OR MUTILATE CURRENCY.

EXPLORER'S CORNER

We are always excited to find coins in an archaeological dig. Since the coins usually have the date and place of minting on them, they are a great indication of the people with whom they were in contact and when. Usually when we find these coins they are corroded, or rusty, and covered with dirt, so we don't know what they mean until long after finding them, when they are finally cleaned.

What happens to coins after they are taken out of circulation? Sometimes coins are melted down or turned into jewelry. Paper money is the most quirky—it simply loses all of its value when discontinued. I could wallpaper my bedroom with all of the discontinued paper money from my travels. Sometimes paper is so devalued that the actual value is less than the material it's made of!

The South African Krugerrand is a gold coin first minted in 1967. It comes in four different sizes, containing 1 ounce, 1/2 ounce, 1/4 ounce, and 1/10 ounce of pure gold. Collectors like this coin because it's worth its weight in gold!

MONEY RETIRES, TOO!

Money gets old and worn out the more it is passed around. Coins last around 25 years in circulation, but most bills don't last more than four to eight years before they are removed from circulation by banks and replaced by crisp new bills. Around the world, collectors hunt for discontinued bills. Currency from the past represents important events, or countries that no longer exist, such as Yugoslavia. As a result, this currency is extremely collectible.

THE WORD "BANK" COMES FROM THE LATIN WORD *BANCO*, FOR THE PORTABLE BENCH ITALIAN MONEY CHANGERS USED AS DESKS FROM ABOUT A.D. 500 TO 1500

HOW TO BE A
BILLIONAIRE

WHO WOULDN'T LIKE TO

MAKE A MOUNTAIN OF MONEY? But earning money isn't easy. The richest people on Earth earn their money in some interesting ways. Many billionaires earned their money by owning a business. Others have had great ideas to offer the world. Still others make their riches as entertainers, athletes, and media tycoons.

Often, people who dream of making big money want all the stuff that goes with it, including a mansion (below). Today's mansions often include private tennis courts, private theaters, swimming pools, elaborate gardens, and even helicopter landing pads.

MONEY WI$E   THE UNITED STATES HAS ABOUT 397 BILLIONAIRES, THE MOST IN THE WORLD, FOLLOWED BY RUSSIA WITH 101.

The Working Life

Most people are not self-made millionaires. They work for companies, the government, or other organizations to make a living. Here are some common professions and their average annual salaries in the United States:

Janitor	$24,120
Secretary	$31,060
Customer Service Representative	$32,000
Accountant	$34,750
Truck Driver	$39,260
Elementary School Teacher	$51,650
Dental Hygienist	$68,000
Operating Room Nurse	$68,473
Civil Engineer	$82,710
Software Developer	$100,420
General Manager/Executive	$110,550
Lawyer	$130,490
Surgeon	$231,550

INVENT A WAY

Cash in, kids! Did you know that the trampoline, earmuffs, and the Popsicle were all invented by kids? And kids keep inventing today. In 2010, Hart Main invented "ManCans," candles made for guys. They smell like such things as grass, baseball mitts, and barbecue. At 15, Christopher Paolini began writing *Eragon*, the first book in the popular series *The Inheritance Cycle*. He invented an imaginative cast of characters that range from elves, to sorcerers, to dragons, and is now a multi-millionaire.

If you invent a product that costs only a couple of dollars to make and then charge a few extra dollars per item, you are making a profit with every item you sell. So, rack your brain for the great ideas.

The Working Life

The richest people in the world are billionaires, people who are worth more than a billion dollars! There are more than 1,225 of them, coming from 58 different countries. They include Bill Gates (above left) and Warren Buffett (above right). Here are the top five and their total worth:

1. Carlos Slim Helú	Mexico	$69 billion	mobile phone company
2. Bill Gates	United States	$61 billion	Microsoft computer software company
3. Warren Buffett	United States	$44 billion	finance, *The World Book Encyclopedia*
4. Bernard Arnault	France	$41 billion	Dior perfume, Louis Vuitton purses and shoes
5. Amancio Ortega	Spain	$37.5 billion	clothing

*Net worth based on 2012 figures

Stock Markets

Who are the people in the picture below, and why are they staring at huge screens? They are stockbrokers at the Saudi Stock Exchange trading large portions of the world's money. Most countries have stock exchanges. A company raises money by selling shares of the company itself, called stocks. Shares cost anywhere from a penny to a few hundred dollars. When you own a share of stock, you are a part owner in the company and earn money as the company does. If the value of the company goes up, you make money! On the flip side, if the value of the company goes down, you lose money.

SPENDING MONEY

WHAT DO PEOPLE
DO WITH ALL THEIR HARD-EARNED MONEY?

A percentage of all income goes to taxes—fees paid to governments to support public services. The amount that is left after taxes is called disposable income. People may spend an average of 40 percent of their disposable income on housing and food. Don't forget about electricity and heat, and your basic transportation needs. What do people do with the money left over?

WHERE THE MONEY GOES

Here are the top twelve things that people spend a lot of their disposable income on:

- groceries
- medical care
- medicine
- furniture and other household items
- food at restaurants
- gas and electric bill
- entertainment
- cars
- TV, music, cable
- housing
- women's clothing
- pets

HOW FAMILIES SPEND MONEY

Entertainment also plays a big role in what families spend. Many families spend about 5 percent of their income on entertainment, such as movies (above) and vacations (below).

MONEY WISE

THE AVERAGE CONSUMER WITH CREDIT CARDS HAS $7,000 WORTH OF DEBT ON THEIR CARDS.

PAY IT FORWARD

Giving money to charity is a way to use your money to help others. The average family gives about 3 percent of their income to charities, according to the U.S. government. Others give away property, such as old clothing or cars. Corporations give even more to charity. With all of the contributions of individuals, foundations, and corporations, over $298 billion is donated to charity annually. The following organizations receive the most donations:

- religious groups
- educational organizations
- human services and disaster relief
- environmental and animal protection
- international charities
- arts and cultural organizations

THE DOOM OF DEBT

There's so much for people to spend money on that many people go into debt by using credit cards and charging more than they can afford to pay back each month. The credit card company charges interest for not paying off the entire bill, so people often see their credit card balances increase instead of shrink. Some people even cut up their credit cards to keep from spending too much.

INVEST

People who invest some disposable income in the stock market may be surprised how their money grows. Suppose you buy 20 shares of Facebook at $20 per share. It costs you $400. Within a few years, the company makes a good profit and the stock price has risen to $50 per share. Your 20 shares are now worth $1,000! But remember that stock investments are risky. The company could have done poorly and its stock price could have gone down to $0.42 per share. Then the shares you spent $400 for would only be worth $8.40. Investing in the stock market can make people win big or lose big.

By the Numbers

$136 BILLION is spent worldwide on sporting equipment.

$122 BILLION is spent worldwide on toys and games.

$85 BILLION is spent worldwide on movie theater tickets.

$75 BILLION is spent worldwide on video games.

$20.8 BILLION is spent worldwide on books and eBooks.

$8.6 BILLION is spent worldwide on digital music recordings.

SAVING MONEY

DOES IT FEEL LIKE YOUR
ALLOWANCE IS BURNING A HOLE IN YOUR
pocket? The urge to spend is hard to resist. Temptations such as music downloads and sweet treats could be strong enough to make you empty your wallet in seconds. But the more you hold on to, the better. If you save a little of your allowance every week, you can save up for the big things you really want.

MONEY WI$E THE U.S. TREASURY ESTIMATES THAT AMERICANS HAVE A TOTAL OF ABOUT $15 BILLION IN LOOSE CHANGE.

GET INTERESTED

The best place to put your money is in the bank (at left). Why? U.S. banks ensure that your money is safe. It is guaranteed up to $250,000, no matter what happens to the physical building or whether the bank can no longer stay in business. And the bank will even pay you interest, a regular payment for keeping your money there. So, a bank is a slow and steady safe bet for your money.

FAMOUS TIGHTWADS

Some people are *really* interested in saving money. A miser is a person who hoards his or her wealth and spends as little as possible. Ebenezer Scrooge (at right), who, in Charles Dickens's *A Christmas Carol* refuses to help the poor and treats his employee unfairly, is a famous fictional miser. However, real-life misers are no less interesting, or stingy! Hetty Green was the richest woman in the world in the early 1900s. Despite her wealth, she lived frugally. She walked to the grocery store and bought broken cookies because they cost less than whole cookies.

PASS IT ON

Sometimes you get lucky and someone else saves money for you. Your parents or grandparents might save money that you could inherit one day. It usually comes from close family members, but not always! One wealthy Portuguese man left his fortune to 70 strangers that he randomly chose from a phone book. Billionaire Leona Helmsley (at right) left $12 million to her pet dog, named Trouble. That's more than she left any of her other family members! Many wealthy people leave money to their pets to ensure that the animals will be cared for after the person is gone.

Some people come into unexpected fortunes. Two homeless brothers from Hungary were living in a cave until they inherited more than a hundred million euros from their grandmother!

A PHOTO GALLERY

THE DESIGNS ON
MONEY OFTEN HIGHLIGHT important national symbols. Currency varies greatly in size, color, and value. Take a look at these currencies from around the globe.

MONEY AROUND THE WORLD

MEXICO

Pesos have been the currency of Mexico since the early 19th century. This bill shows the Mexican coat of arms—an eagle with a snake in its beak perched on a cactus.

BRAZIL

Brazil's currency is called a real. The backs of the bills have images of different animals that live in the country, such as the hawksbill turtle.

ANTARCTICA

Few people live in Antarctica. Its dollars are not legal currency but are collector's items. Each denomination has a different theme. The one-dollar bill has an Adélie penguin theme, and the twenty-dollar bill has an explorer theme.

RUSSIA

This 1995 ten-ruble note features a picture of a famous bridge across the Yenisei River and the Chapel of Saint Paraskeva Pyatnitsa. While this bill is still in circulation, it is less widely available.

THAILAND

Thailand's currency is called the baht. At the top left of this ten-baht note is an image of the Garuda, a mythological creature from Hindu and Buddhist tradition.

ETHIOPIA

Ethiopia's currency is called the birr. The one-birr note features an image of oxen, which are widely used to cultivate crops in the country.

ZIMBABWE

Zimbabwe once had a bill worth 100 trillion Zimbabwean dollars. But the bill, worth only about five dollars in U.S. currency, was discontinued in 2009. The Chiremba Balancing Rocks in Harare, shown on the front of the bill, symbolize the importance of balancing the environment with modern development.

Companies set up offices and plants in cities around the world, such as Tokyo (pictured). Big companies help the local and global economies by employing workers and creating goods and services that people buy.

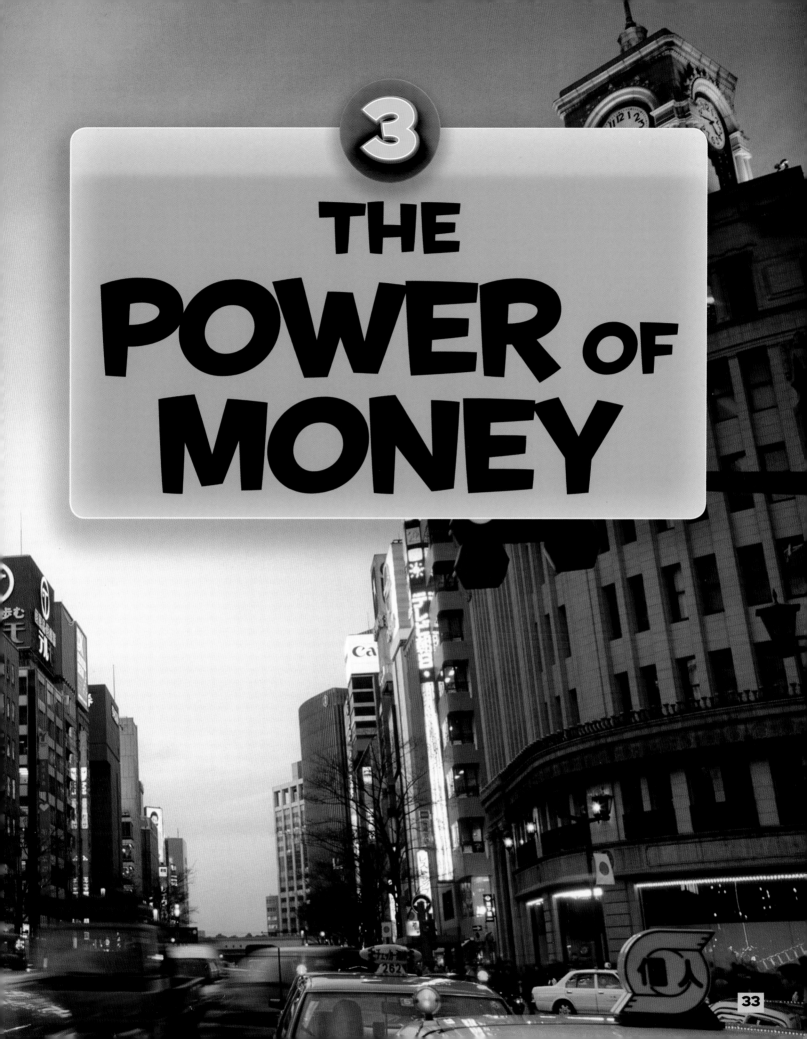

3

THE POWER OF MONEY

MONEY IN THE WORLD

THIS MAP
SHOWS THE RICHEST
and poorest countries in the world. A country's wealth is determined by the value of its currency and its living standards. One aspect of a country's living standard is its gross domestic product, or GDP. This figure is the total value of all the goods and services that a country creates. Rich countries have a high GDP while poor countries have a low GDP.

Currencies of the Richest and Poorest Countries

LIECHTENSTEIN

Swiss franc

QATAR

Qatari riyal

LUXEMBOURG

Euro

SINGAPORE

Singapore dollar

NORWAY

Norwegian krone

SOMALIA

Somali shilling

BURUNDI

Burundian franc

ZIMBABWE

Zimbabwean dollar*

LIBERIA

Liberian dollar

DEMOCRATIC REPUBLIC OF THE CONGO

Congolese franc

*Due to extreme inflation, the Zimbabwean dollar's use was mostly discontinued in early 2009. Zimbabwe now uses foreign currencies such as the U.S. dollar and the South African rand, among others.

LUXEMBOURG

LIBERIA

The Five

MONEY WI$E
THE FACE OF GREAT BRITAIN'S QUEEN ELIZABETH II HAS BEEN ON THE CURRENCY OF 33 COUNTRIES.

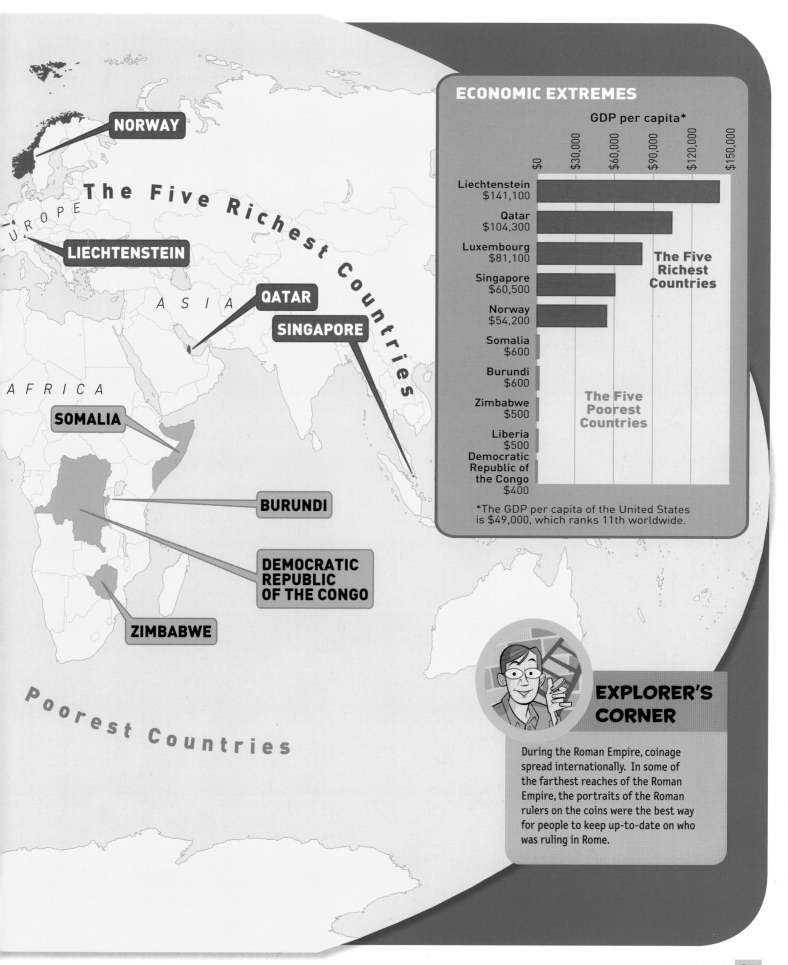

NORWAY

The Five Richest Countries

EUROPE

LIECHTENSTEIN

ASIA

QATAR

SINGAPORE

AFRICA

SOMALIA

BURUNDI

DEMOCRATIC
REPUBLIC
OF THE CONGO

ZIMBABWE

Poorest Countries

ECONOMIC EXTREMES

GDP per capita*

$0 $30,000 $60,000 $90,000 $120,000 $150,000

Liechtenstein
$141,100

Qatar
$104,300

Luxembourg
$81,100

The Five Richest Countries

Singapore
$60,500

Norway
$54,200

Somalia
$600

Burundi
$600

The Five Poorest Countries

Zimbabwe
$500

Liberia
$500

Democratic Republic of the Congo
$400

*The GDP per capita of the United States is $49,000, which ranks 11th worldwide.

EXPLORER'S CORNER

During the Roman Empire, coinage spread internationally. In some of the farthest reaches of the Roman Empire, the portraits of the Roman rulers on the coins were the best way for people to keep up-to-date on who was ruling in Rome.

MONEY EXTREMES

PEOPLE DREAM OF HAVING SO
MUCH CASH THEY DON'T KNOW WHAT TO DO WITH IT.

People who do have tons of cash find some unusual thngs to spend it on, from a 27-story skyscraper to a $16 million racehorse to the world's largest diamond. What would you buy if money were no object?

WORLD'S PRICIEST HOME

A wealthy Indian businessman spent $2 billion to have a 27-story skyscraper built for himself in downtown Mumbai, India. It's the world's most expensive house!

MOST VALUABLE TREASURE

In 2005, adventurers discovered the biggest pirates' treasure ever found—600 barrels of gold coins and Inca jewels—on a remote island in the Pacific Ocean. The loot, valued at around $10 billion, had been buried around 1715 by Spanish sailor Juan Esteban Ubilla y Echeverría. The treasure was finally found with the help of a robot that had advanced sensors.

MOST EXPENSIVE RACEHORSE

A 12-year-old Thoroughbred racehorse named the Green Monkey was purchased for $16 million in 2006. The price was so high because she was descended from two Kentucky Derby winners. Unfortunately, she ended up being a flop on the track. It was the highest price ever paid for a horse.

THE LARGEST DIAMOND

The biggest diamond ever found is 3,106 carats and has an estimated value of $400 million. Known as the Cullinan Diamond, it was cut into smaller pieces. The largest of the pieces is named the Great Star of Africa (right). This 530-carat diamond sits atop the Scepter of the Cross, which is part of the British Crown Jewels. During coronations, the monarch holds the scepter in his or her right hand.

MONEY WI$E YOU CAN PURCHASE A DIAMOND COLLAR FOR YOUR DOG THAT COSTS UP TO $480,000.

MONEY IN THE DIGITAL AGE

IN TODAY'S WORLD YOU CAN

BUY A NEW VIDEO GAME, PAY THE ELECTRIC BILL, and get paid for walking your neighbor's poodle all without touching a single bill or coin. They electronically take money from your bank account to pay for items. Credit cards are accepted worldwide. You can transfer money between accounts on a computer, and you can wire money across the world instantly. Do we really need cash anymore?

DOLLARS AND SENSE

It is easy to lose track of how much money you have spent using a debit or credit card. Many banks charge steep fines when there is not enough money in an account to cover debit card purchases. Luckily, you can check your bank balance online to see how much money you have—before you go shopping!

MAKING THE TRADE

Before computers, the entire stock exchange used to operate with brokers carrying paper tickets around to make trades. Today, that has all been replaced by computers. People can now make their own trades online or on the phone instead of using brokers.

CYBER SHOPPING

For decades, the day after Thanksgiving, known as Black Friday, was the biggest shopping day of the year. Now there's Cyber Monday, the Monday following Thanksgiving and the biggest online shopping day of the year. On this day, people in the United States use laptops, tablets, and cell phones to buy gifts from online stores. In 2011, Cyber Monday brought in $1.25 billion for retailers.

GET MONEY 24/7

Need cash? The ATM, or automated teller machine, makes it simple to get money at any time of the day or night. Using your bank card in the ATM, you can withdraw cash from your bank account nearly everywhere in the world. For example, you can get euros from an ATM in France or rupees from an ATM in India.

PAY FOR VIDEO GAMES WITH YOUR PHONE?

Debit and credit cards aren't the only ways to pay for things without cash. There are apps for smartphones that allow shoppers to buy and sell things without ever opening their wallets. These apps automatically add or subtract money from a person's bank account as soon as the person pushes the buy or sell button.

MONEY WI$E THE FIRST ATM WAS USED IN ENGLAND IN 1967.

CRIMES, HEISTS, AND SCAMS

FROM THE EARLY DAYS OF TRAIN ROBBERIES
TO MODERN BANK HEISTS, SOME PEOPLE HAVE DONE CRAZY THINGS TO GET

fast cash. Stealing money can have harsh punishments, including long prison sentences. But that didn't stop these crafty crooks from committing these famous crimes.

During the 19th century in America, railroads became more popular as a way of traveling—and as a target for robberies. The exploits of outlaws, such as Jesse James or the Dalton gang, were later captured in movies such as the 1939 film *Union Pacific* (below).

STOLEN TREASURES

A burglar broke into the National Museum of Modern Art in Paris in 2010 and stole five paintings, including a Matisse and a Picasso (at right). The value of the paintings was about 100 million euros, which is about 131 million U.S. dollars. The paintings are still missing, and the thief was never found.

Henri Matisse, "Pastoral," 1905

Pablo Picasso, "Dove with Green Peas," 1911

IS THAT YOU?

An identity thief could be someone who steals your credit card and charges goods under your name. It could also be someone who uses another person's identity to commit another kind of crime, such as terrorism, drug trafficking, or computer or cyber crimes. It can often be difficult to prove that your identity has been stolen and that you did not commit those crimes yourself, so it is important for people to protect their financial and personal identity as much as possible.

By the Numbers

$1 TRILLION
annual amount lost worldwide from Internet fraud

$221 BILLION
annual amount lost to businesses worldwide due to identity theft

$500 MILLION
annual U.S. amount spent to help victims of theft

$456 MILLION
annual losses attributed to U.S. robberies

$3.5 MILLION
losses due to worldwide car thefts each year

$2,119
average loss per U.S. burglary

MONEY WI$E THERE ARE ABOUT TEN MILLION VICTIMS OF IDENTITY THEFT PER YEAR.

PRICE COMPARISONS

THE COST OF LIVING

HOW MUCH DID IT COST IN 1951?

HOW MUCH DOES IT COST TODAY?

Most of the time, the cost of things such as cars or computers increases because the cost of the materials used to make those things increases. With each year, prices continue to rise. It's a good thing that salaries increase over the years as well. In fact, people earn larger salaries in order to keep up with increases in the cost of living. Take a look at how the cost of things in the United States has changed since 1951. The prices are averages for each time period.

1951: $9,000

VS.

2012: $177,000

GALLON OF GASOLINE

1951: 19¢

VS.

2012: $3.50

NEW CAR

1951: $1,500   VS.   2012: $29,000

LOAF OF BREAD

1951: 16¢   VS.   2012: $1.98

MEAT FOR FOUR HAMBURGERS

1951: 50¢   VS.   2012: $3.30

More than 250 million people around the world have played the board game Monopoly since it was published in 1935. Players try to "get rich" by buying property. The game was developed by Charles Darrow, who had lost his job after the 1929 stock market crash and later became a millionaire after Parker Brothers purchased the game in 1935.

4

FUN WITH MONEY

KNOW YOUR MONEY

MONEY COMES UP A LOT IN

EVERYDAY CONVERSATIONS. BUT DO PEOPLE REALLY know what they are talking about? From myths about savings to popular sayings, everyone has an opinion about money.

MONEY MYTHS

MYTH: If you find money on the ground, it is yours to keep.

FACT: Laws are a little different across territories, but the majority of them say that money still belongs to its owner, not its finder. However, in Canada, the United States, Great Britain, and many other countries, if the owner does not claim the money, the person who found it cashes in!

MYTH: Banks are not safe for saving money.

FACT: Money is safest in a bank. In fact, the U.S. government insures up to $250,000 in an account, which means if the bank was robbed or went out of business, the government would write you a check!

MYTH: The only currency is bills and coins.

FACT: Postage stamps are, by law, considered currency. They are made by the government and have a value, just like bills and coins. However, most stores won't take stamps as payment, so cash is still best.

© BCE ECB EZB EKT EKP 2002

500 EURO EYPΩ

MONEY WI$E   IN 2010 THE INDIAN GOVERNMENT HELD A CONTEST TO DESIGN A SYMBOL FOR THE RUPEE.

BE WORLDLY ABOUT MONEY

Using the symbols on the money as hints, match each bill below to the correct name of its currency.

1

2

3

4

5

A  £ British pound

B  ₹ Indian rupee

C  ¥ Japanese yen

D  ₩ Korean won

E  $ Canadian dollar

EXCHANGE YOUR CHANGE

If you travel to Europe or Japan, how will you know how much your dollars are worth? The exchange rate tells us how much money in one currency is worth in another. For example, a U.S. dollar has a different value from a euro or a Japanese yen. To compare values, first establish the amount of the currency you wish to convert to the second currency. Establish the current exchange rate between the two currencies. Multiply the amount of the first currency by the exchange rate. This will tell you the equivalent amount of money in the second currency. For example, the chart below tells you that 10 dollars equals 781 yen, so 100 dollars would be ten times that. To convert 100 dollars to yen, multiply 10 times 781, which equals 7,810 yen. Now you try!

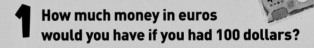

2012 VALUES

10.00 DOLLARS = 8.12 EURO = 781 YEN

1 How much money in euros would you have if you had 100 dollars?

2 If something costs 50 dollars, how much would it cost in yen?

3 Who would have more money:
A. an American with 50 dollars
B. a European with 390 euros
C. a Japanese person with 4,000 yen

YOU CAN SAY THAT AGAIN

Here are some famous sayings about money.

"Money often costs too much."
—Ralph Waldo Emerson, poet (1803–1882)

"Never spend your money before you have it."
—Thomas Jefferson, American president (1743–1826)

"I don't care too much for money, 'cause money can't buy me love."
—The Beatles, rock band (1960–1975)

MONEY ORIGAMI

FOLLOW THESE DIRECTIONS TO
FOLD A DOLLAR BILL INTO AN ORIGAMI BUTTERFLY.

1 Fold in half and unfold.

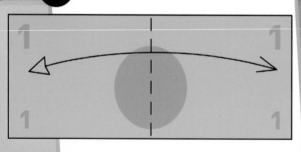

2 Fold both corners to the center along the dotted lines.

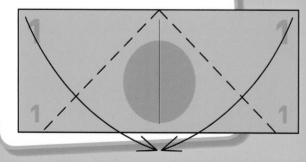

3

Turn over.

4 Fold the outer edges along the dotted lines so they meet in the center.

Used with the permission of John Montroll, the author of several origami books, including *Dollar Bill Origami, Dollar Origami Treasures, Easy Dollar Bill Origami,* and the Fun Dollar Origami app for iPhone.

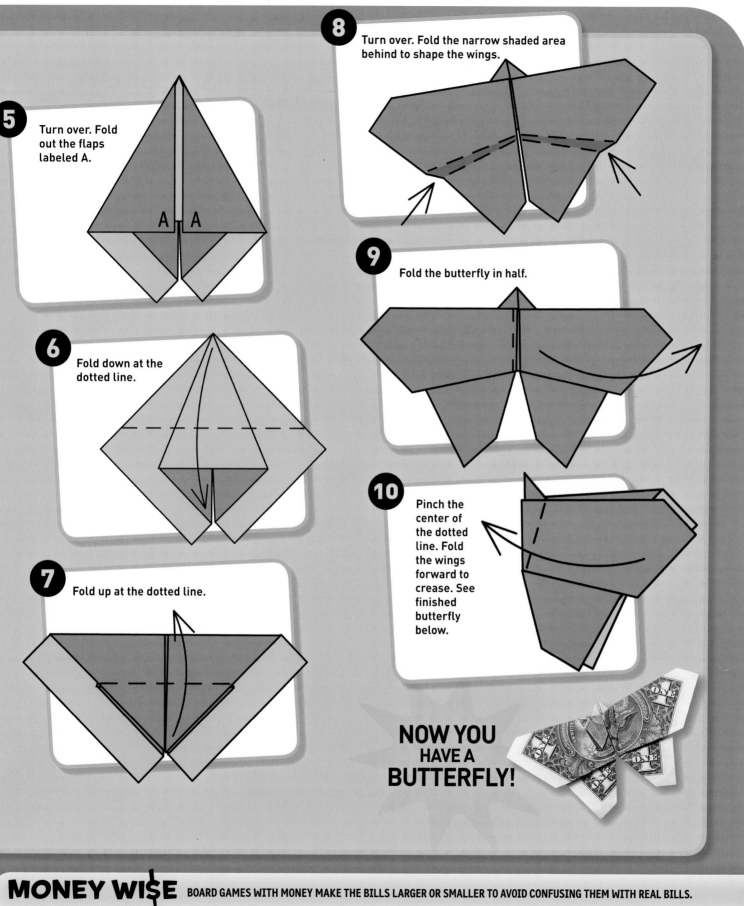

5 Turn over. Fold out the flaps labeled A.

A A

6 Fold down at the dotted line.

7 Fold up at the dotted line.

8 Turn over. Fold the narrow shaded area behind to shape the wings.

9 Fold the butterfly in half.

10 Pinch the center of the dotted line. Fold the wings forward to crease. See finished butterfly below.

NOW YOU HAVE A BUTTERFLY!

COIN COLLECTOR'S PARADISE

COIN COLLECTING IS A HOBBY FOR

PEOPLE ALL AROUND THE WORLD. COLLECTING CAN BE A serious business, too. People buy and sell coins based on the coins' condition. A coin is most valuable in "mint" condition, which means it looks brand new and probably was never used as money. It is least valuable in "poor" condition, which means the details are worn down and hard to see.

MONEY WI$E   SOME 1969 U.S. PENNIES MINTED WITH ERRORS ARE WORTH OVER $30,000.

50

CHECK YOUR POCKETS

Alert! Always be on the lookout for rare coins! For example, ancient Greek coins called tetradrachms that feature the portrait of Alexander the Great are valued for their historical significance. They were minted between 356 B.C. and 326 B.C.! Other coins go up in value because of printing errors, such as extra images, missing letters, or missing dates. For example, there is a rare printing of the 2004 Wisconsin state quarter with an extra leaf printed on the left side of the corn husk. The look was caused by an accident. If you've got that quarter in your pocket, it can be worth up to $300.

Another valuable coin is a U.S. half-dollar printed before 1964. These coins contain 90 percent silver, so they are worth a whole lot more than 50 cents! The British 20-pence coin is a collector's item because it's missing its date. The coin, originally valued at a fraction of a British pound, is now valued at £100 ($161 U.S.).

Greek tetradrachm

2004 Wisconsin state quarter

U.S. silver half-dollar

British 20-pence coin

COLLECTING COINS

People collect coins for their historical connections and beauty. For many collectors it's a fun hobby, and they don't expect to earn a profit from their collections. However, the most valuable coins belong in museums so everyone can enjoy them. Visitors to the Michael C. Ruettgers Gallery for Ancient Coins in Boston, Massachusetts, U.S.A., can examine details of ancient Greek and Roman coins under moveable magnifying glasses and design their own coins. At the British Museum in London, England, coin lovers can trace the history of money back 4,000 years. Another popular collection that was housed at the Egyptian Museum in Cairo, Egypt, below, contained a collection that included rare coins from the 600s B.C.—the first ever made!

EXPLORER'S CORNER

In 1984, underwater archaeologist Barry Clifford found the first real pirate ship-wreck. The ship, called the *Whydah*, was taken over by pirates in the Caribbean and sank off of Cape Cod, Massachusetts, U.S.A., in 1717. Clifford discovered over 10,000 coins and 400 pieces of gold jewelry on board. Many of the artifacts are displayed at a museum in Provincetown, Massachusetts, and nothing will be sold. The ship's history is its real treasure!

BUDGETING AND BARTERING

EASY COME, EASY GO—
THAT'S ONE WAY TO LOOK AT MONEY.

However, budgeting your money helps you make sure you don't waste it on things you want instead of things you need. For example, if you spend all of your money on snacks, you won't have enough for new soccer cleats. A budget is a written plan for how to use your money. To create a budget, record how much money you have coming in each month from odd jobs, allowance, or gifts. Then record what you will spend it on.

Bartering, on the other hand, is a way to get goods and services without spending actual money. Do you have a special skill, such as babysitting? Trade your services for something you need, such as homework help. Then everybody wins!

OR ???

2. $4.29

1. $16.79

TAX BREAK

A sales tax is the tax that is added to the things we buy, such as clothes or electronics. Most countries have some sort of sales tax, which can range from 5 percent to as high as 30 percent. In the United States, states set their own sales tax. Sales tax generally pays for state and government services, including everything from education to paying for firefighters and paving roads. Calculate the total price of number 1 and 2 by adding a 6 percent sales tax. First, multiply the price of the item by 0.06. Then, add that amount to the price to get the final cost.

1. Price after tax: _____

2. Price after tax: _____

GIFT GIVING!

It's time to buy presents for three of your friends. Think about the items that you just added tax to. Then figure out how much it would cost (with tax!) to buy three of each item.

MONEY WI$E THE WORLD'S MOST VALUABLE TRADING CARD IS A 1909 HONUS WAGNER BASEBALL CARD WORTH $3,000,000.

52 NGK EVERYTHING

a. $201.18

b. $86.33

A SMARTER BARTER

You scored a valuable rookie trading card worth $299. Good job! The owner of your local sporting goods store will barter goods from his store for the card. Choose the two items on this page that add up to exactly $299.

c. $96.32

d. $500

e. $202.68

A PHOTO FINISH

ARCHAEOLOGISTS ARE LIKE

DETECTIVES, SEARCHING FOR CLUES. WE CAN actually trace activities and events back hundreds and thousands of years!

The past can be seen everywhere, even today. I took this picture several years ago in a market in the Middle East. The market is made up of dozens of stalls like this one, called souks. Just about everything in this shop is made in China, and it reminded me of my very first archaeological expedition.

In that dig, not far from the market in the picture, we were looking for clues to the first trade from China to Arabia, which took place thousands of years ago. In the modern shop, they were selling fancy dishes from China. In the archaeological site, we found ancient fancy dishes from China, and we also found ancient money.

We dug near the coast and found the walls of a huge fortified warehouse for traded goods. Around the gates, we found a lot of broken pottery and metal pieces from ships. But the most amazing find was a handful of copper coins, probably lost by merchants conducting business in the warehouse. Some of the coins had been minted in Persia and Arabia, but most of the coins were Chinese. They had Chinese writing on them and a square hole in the middle. These coins were common in China, but finding these coins in Arabia makes this an important discovery. It proves that Chinese traders had traveled all the way across the Indian Ocean more than a thousand years ago! Today, the coins are in a museum in Manama, Bahrain.

We think that the ancient Chinese traders bought spices, glass, and perhaps perfume made in Arabia and sailed back to China with these goods—just as international tourists shop at modern souks today, returning home with such souvenirs as spices, leather, and books.

AFTERWORD

DOES SOMEONE NEED TO

BE RICH TO BE A PHILANTHROPIST? NOT A chance. There are plenty of people who raise modest sums of money for a good cause, and some of those people are even kids! Some kids look around and naturally see places where they can improve the way that some people live. They may see people living without basic necessities, or they may wish to help animals or the environment. Whatever it is, they feel the need to give back to the community in important ways.

Timothy Hwang and Minsoo Han started an organization called Operation Fly when they were 14 years old. They offered inexpensive tutoring services to inner-city kids who were struggling in school. Then they took the money they earned and bought basic necessities for the city's homeless, including blankets, soap, and clothing. Since they started it in 2007, the organization has spread to other cities, is entirely run by students, and has more than 800 volunteers.

At ten years old, Talia Leman saw the devastation of Hurricane Katrina on the news. Hurricane Katrina struck the Gulf Coast of the United States in late August 2005. Katrina was among the country's top five deadliest hurricanes. Talia began collecting coins to help the hurricane victims, and she hasn't stopped fundraising since. Today, her organization, RandomKid, provides kids who have ideas for philanthropic projects the ability to turn their ideas into reality. The organization has built schools around the globe and provided storm-damaged communities with clean drinking water, among other projects. Kids develop all of the ideas and work with others to put them in motion. A little innovation can go a long way. Random-Kid has worked with more than 12 million children from 20 countries. That's a big business of giving!

Talia Leman began collecting money for victims of Hurricane Katrina, which struck the U.S. Gulf Coast in 2005. Today, she leads an organization called RandomKid, which helps other students organize philanthropy projects. In the photo above, Talia uses a map to keep track of organizations she is helping.

HOW CAN YOU RAISE MONEY FOR A GOOD CAUSE?

First, brainstorm ideas about what you want to do to raise the money. Then write a plan of action to decide what the money will do to help your community. Does your plan help the residents or homeless in your local community? Take your plan to the mayor's office. Does it help the environment? Try talking to a local environmental group. Does it help sick people? Try a local hospital. Bring your idea and your funds to the place that can reach the most people.

My Plan
Collect money to start curbside recycling program. Drive bottles to recycling center.

Collect old blankets for homeless. Start laundry system to clean blankets.

Men, women, and children take part in the annual Braughing Wheelbarrow Race in Braughing, England, to raise money for charity.

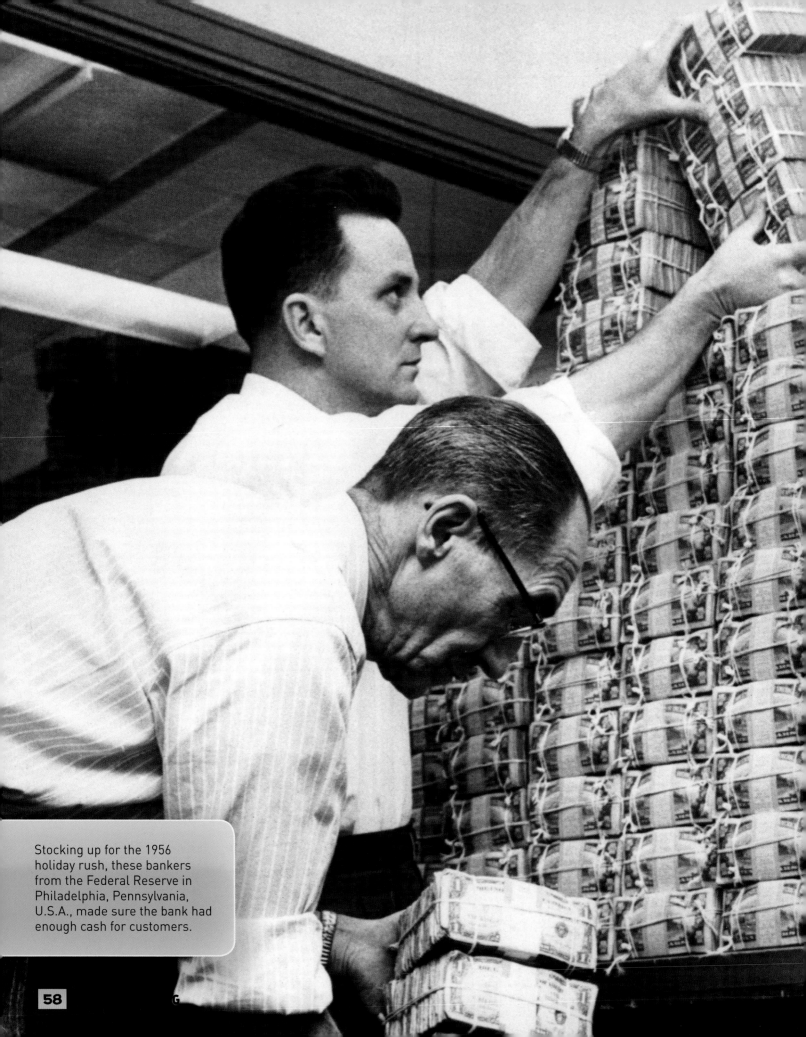

Stocking up for the 1956 holiday rush, these bankers from the Federal Reserve in Philadelphia, Pennsylvania, U.S.A., made sure the bank had enough cash for customers.

AN INTERACTIVE GLOSSARY

A Mercedes studded with 300,000 Swarovski crystals is just one of many custom cars at the annual Tokyo Auto Salon. The car is valued at a whopping $1 million.

THESE WORDS ARE

COMMONLY USED to talk about money. Use the glossary to learn what each word means and visit its page numbers to see the word used in context. Then test your money knowledge!

Barter
(PAGES 10–11)
the exchange of goods and services for other goods and services

What is another word for a barter?
a. tax
b. budget
c. loan
d. trade

Budget
(PAGES 52–53)
a plan for how money should be spent

Living on a budget can help people ___ money.
a. save
b. counterfeit
c. lose
d. earn

Counterfeiting
(PAGES 18–19)
the illegal act of making unofficial currency

How are counterfeiters often punished?
a. bank
b. jail
c. stock exchange
d. department store

Cowrie Shell
(PAGES 12–13)
one of the earliest and most common forms of currency

Cowrie shells come from ___.
a. bird eggs
b. mollusks
c. lobsters
d. turtles

Currency
(PAGES 10–11)
a system of money used by a particular country or region

Which is NOT an example of currency?
a. a goat for bartering
b. silver coins
c. paper money
d. a loan from a bank

Cyber Monday
(PAGES 38–39)
one of the biggest online shopping days of the year

What day is Cyber Monday?
a. the day before Christmas
b. Memorial Day
c. the first Monday after the U.S. Thanksgiving holiday
d. the first day of school

Debt
(PAGES 26–27)
the amount of money that a person owes to others

How can people go into debt?
a. by earning more money than they need
b. by saving more money than they spend
c. by spending exactly what they earn
d. by borrowing more money than they can pay back

Inheritance
(PAGES 28–29)
money or other valuables received by someone after its previous owner has died

Most people leave their inheritance to their ___.
a. family members
b. banks
c. stock brokers
d. lawyers

Interest
(PAGES 26–27)
additional money owed to a creditor or investor at a particular rate on top of the original loan or investment.

How can people avoid paying interest?
a. by buying only small items with a credit card
b. by paying a small amount of the balance each month
c. by buying only expensive items with a credit card
d. by paying off the full balance each month

Loan
(PAGES 10–11)
something that is borrowed with a promise that it will be paid back at a later time

Where do people most often go to get a loan?
a. gas station
b. bank
c. grocery store
d. school

Philanthropist
(PAGES 56–57)
a person who helps others by donating money

Which types of donations do philanthropists most typically make?
a. homemade food
b. check
c. old toys
d. homework help

Stock
(PAGES 24–25)
a share, or part ownership, in a company

A person buys stock in a company in hope of ___ money.
a. losing
b. making
c. lending
d. sharing

Stockbroker
(PAGES 24–25)
a person who buys and sells stocks on behalf of clients

Where do most stockbrokers work?
a. at a credit card company
b. in a mall
c. at a stock exchange
d. at a bank

Tax
(PAGES 26–27)
an amount of money that citizens pay to their government

Income taxes are usually taken out of people's ___.
a. piggy banks
b. paychecks
c. wallets
d. mattresses

Wampum
(PAGES 12–13)
beads used as currency by Native Americans between the 1400s and 1700s

What did people use wampum to pay for?
a. food
b. housing
c. animal hides
d. all of the above

FIND OUT MORE

Invest in more knowledge about money with these websites, games, and books.

MONEY SITES

usmint.gov/kids
H.I.P. Pocket Change is the official kids' site of the U.S. Mint, which includes tons of information about commemorative coins, money, history, and news about the Mint.

orangekids.com
Planet Orange is a kids' website about earning, spending, saving, and investing money, sponsored by ING Direct.

zefty.com
Zefty.com is a system that allows parents and kids to track and manage a child's allowance and spending online.

richkidsmartkid.com/index.html
Rich Kid Smart Kid is a website that teaches about debt, spending, and saving money.

MONEY GAMES

Financial Football
Visit practicalmoneyskills.com/games/trainingcamp/ff to give yourself a financial workout.

The Game of Life
Hasbro Gaming, Inc.
Find out whether you will end up in the millionaire's mansion or the retirement home in this classic board game.

Mad Money
Visit pbskids.org/itsmylife/money/index.html to play this interactive game of budgeting and spending.

Monopoly
Hasbro Gaming, Inc.
Gather a fortune in this popular real-estate game.

MONEY BOOKS

A Kid's Guide to Collecting Coins
BY ARLYN G. SIEBER
Krause Publications, 2011
An easy-to-follow guide to coin collecting and finding the value of coins.

World's Greatest Mint Errors
BY MIKE BYERS
Zyrus Press, 2009
A fascinating guide to major mint errors around the world.

PLACES TO VISIT

Bank of England Museum
London, England

Citi Money Gallery at the British Museum
London, England

United States Treasury
Washington, D.C., U.S.A.

Money Museum
Colorado Springs, Colorado, U.S.A.

For Ben and Caleb. —KF

Acknowledgments: A special thanks to Fred Hiebert, National Geographic Explorer-in-Residence, and Thomas Hockenhull for reviewing the text.

Published by the National Geographic Society
John M. Fahey, *Chairman of the Board and Chief Executive Officer*
Tim Kelly, *President*
Declan Moore, *Executive Vice President; President, Publishing and Digital Media*
Melina Gerosa Bellows, *Executive Vice President; Chief Creative Officer, Books, Kids, and Family*

Prepared by the Book Division
Hector Sierra, *Senior Vice President and General Manager*
Nancy Laties Feresten, *Senior Vice President, Kids Publishing and Media*
Jonathan Halling, *Design Director, Books and Children's Publishing*
Jay Sumner, *Director of Photography, Children's Publishing*
Jennifer Emmett, *Vice President, Editorial Director, Children's Books*
Eva Absher-Schantz, *Design Director, Kids Publishing and Media*
Carl Mehler, *Director of Maps*
R. Gary Colbert, *Production Director*
Jennifer A. Thornton, *Director of Managing Editorial*

Staff for This Book
Robin Terry, *Project Manager*
James Hiscott, Jr., *Art Director*
Lori Epstein, *Senior Illustrations Editor*
Ariane Szu-Tu, *Editorial Assistant*
Kathryn Robbins, *Associate Designer*
Hillary Moloney, *Illustrations Assistant*
Grace Hill, *Associate Managing Editor*
Joan Gossett, *Production Editor*
Lewis R. Bassford, *Production Manager*
Susan Borke, *Legal and Business Affairs*

Manufacturing and Quality Management
Phillip L. Schlosser, *Senior Vice President*
Chris Brown, *Vice President, NG Book Manufacturing*
George Bounelis, *Vice President, Production Services*
Nicole Elliott, *Manager*
Rachel Faulise, *Manager*
Robert L. Barr, *Manager*

Design and Production by Q2A/Bill Smith

Captions
Page 1: Small money banks, such as this piggy bank, have been used for more than 2,000 years.
Pages 2–3: Most people wish money would rain from the sky.

The National Geographic Society is one of the world's largest nonprofit scientific and educational organizations. Founded in 1888 to "increase and diffuse geographic knowledge," the Society works to inspire people to care about the planet. National Geographic reflects the world through its magazines, television programs, films, music and radio, books, DVDs, maps, exhibitions, live events, school publishing programs, interactive media and merchandise. *National Geographic* magazine, the Society's official journal, published in English and 33 local-language editions, is read by more than 60 million people each month. The National Geographic Channel reaches 435 million households in 37 languages in 173 countries. National Geographic Digital Media receives more than 19 million visitors a month. National Geographic has funded more than 10,000 scientific research, conservation, and exploration projects and supports an education program promoting geography literacy. For more information, visit nationalgeographic.com.

For more information, please call 1-800-NGS LINE (647-5463) or write to the following address:
National Geographic Society
1145 17th Street N.W.
Washington, D.C. 20036-4688 U.S.A.

Visit us online at www.nationalgeographic.com/books

For librarians and teachers: www.ngchildrensbooks.org

More for kids from National Geographic:
kids.nationalgeographic.com

For information about special discounts for bulk purchases, please contact National Geographic Books Special Sales: ngspecsales@ngs.org

For rights or permissions inquiries, please contact National Geographic Books Subsidiary Rights: ngbookrights@ngs.org

Library of Congress Cataloging-in-Publication Data
Furgang, Kathy.
Everything money: a wealth of facts, photos, and fun! / by Kathy Furgang.
   p. cm.
Includes bibliographical references and index.
ISBN 978-1-4263-1026-3 (pbk. : alk. paper)—ISBN 978-1-4263-1027-0 (library binding : alk. paper)
1. Money—History—Juvenile literature. I. Title.
HG221.5.F87 2013
332.4'9—dc23
                                    2012023785
Printed in China
13/TS/1